HOLIDAY DECORATING

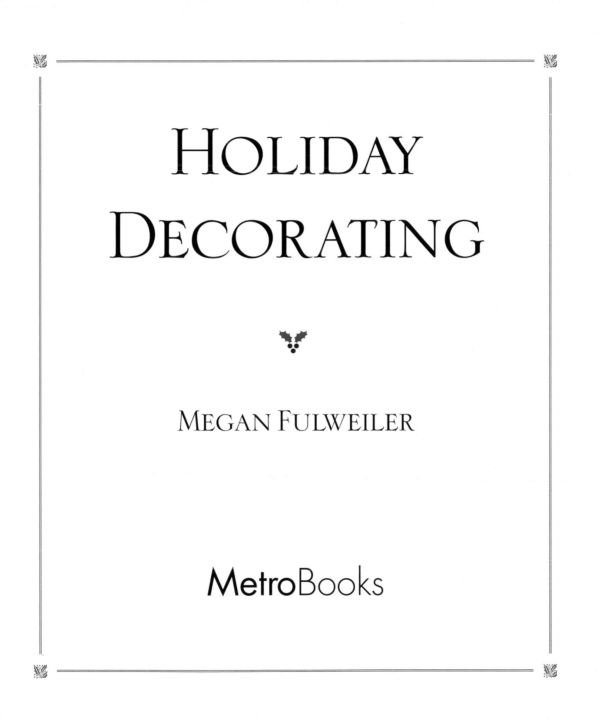

HOLIDAY DECORATING

MEGAN FULWEILER

MetroBooks

MetroBooks

An Imprint of Friedman/Fairfax Publishers

Library of Congress Cataloging-in-Publication Data

Fulweiler, Megan.
    Holiday decorating / Megan Fulweiler.
        p. cm.
    Includes index.
    ISBN 1-58663-227-2
    1. Christmas decorations–United States. 2. Interior decoration–United States. I. Title.

NK2115.5.C45 F85 2001
398.2663–dc21

2001030818

Editor: Hallie Einhorn
Art Director: Jeff Batzli
Designer: Midori Nakamura
Photo Editor: Jami Ruszkai
Production Manager: Richela Fabian Morgan

Color separations by Radstock Repro
Printed in England by Butler & Tanner Ltd.

1 3 5 7 9 10 8 6 4 2

For bulk purchases and special sales, please contact:
Friedman/Fairfax Publishers
Attention: Sales Department
230 Fifth Avenue
New York, NY 10001
212/685-6610 FAX 212/685-3916

Visit our website:
www.metrobooks.com

CONTENTS

INTRODUCTION

Deck the halls! In the weeks leading up to Christmas, we open our homes and our hearts to friends and family with a fervor that comes only once a year. While this is a time to revisit favorite traditions, it is also a time to try new things and let our imaginations soar. Maybe this December we'll decide to adorn the tree with colorful lights or dress the dining table in shades of gold. Perhaps we'll plant the poinsettias in silver pots or dangle antique ornaments from the chandelier. There's an almost infinite number of creative possibilities for reinventing our famil-iar spaces so that each and every one—from the foyer to the family room—becomes an invitation to linger, savor the season, and revel in the unending wonder of Christmas.

Give your home—be it a simple farmhouse or an elegant city apartment—your own personal holiday stamp and watch how it shines. With a spellbinding combination of old ideas and new, you can fashion a host of merry, magical memories to last you—and all those you love— a lifetime.

OPPOSITE: *Home is the center of our holiday celebrations. Enhance the festivi-ties by bringing some decorative touches to both the exterior and interior of your home.*

First Impressions

❦

Outdoor decorations are a joyous pronouncement to the world that the holiday spirit is officially upon us. Whether you prefer a simple statement, such as a welcoming wreath posted on the front door, or an elaborate declaration, perhaps a dazzling light show complete with a candle in every window and twinkling white lights strung across the trees, there are numerous ways to send your best holiday wishes.

❧ Green Merrymaking ❧

Nothing heralds Christmas like a front door wearing a fresh green wreath. It's a classic statement that never gets old. Forgo the plastic reindeer and the garish blinking lights; wreaths are timeless greetings of peace on earth, goodwill toward men.

There are numerous choices when it comes to wreaths. These ancient circular symbols of life and love can be made from a wide variety of natural materials, including juniper, hemlock, fir, holly, arborvitae, laurel, and magnolia, to name a few. Hang a simple wreath fashioned

OPPOSITE: Like a blank canvas, the exterior of a home lends itself to decoration. Here, white lights strung along the fence and second-floor railings, along with a wealth of beribboned wreaths and garlands, transform the scene into a Christmas wonderland.

from the cuttings of just one plant or a sumptuous wreath composed of several plants for a more opulent effect. Glossy boxwood is the perfect exclamation point for a stately Colonial door framed with sidelights and columns; sassy bittersweet vine entwined with ivy is fitting for a simple, painted door. But there are no real rules with regard to wreaths. Whether suspended on a door, wall, or window (inside or out), the wreath has as many variations as fruitcake. Make yours a banner of your own individual Christmas style.

A SEASON OF SYMBOLS

Long ago, plants were chosen for wreaths and garlands according to their symbolism. Perpetually green ivy, for instance, was considered a token of love and everlasting life. Holly, perhaps the most revered holiday plant of all because of its ability to bear fruit in winter, was thought to repel witches and entice beneficial spirits into the home. Pungent rosemary, an emblem of eternity, stood for remembrance.

While a fragrant, unadorned wreath is a splendid sight, there are many possibilities for added embellishment. Wreaths decked out with everything from pinecones to bright red chili peppers will extend a heartfelt welcome. Indeed, wreaths can be teamed with all sorts of inspired ingredients. Fresh fruit—such as lemons, kumquats, and

clementines—can float jewellike amid the greenery; such other natural finds as nuts, dried flowers, seedpods, and twigs can be woven in for a woodland feel. Think of each wreath as a blank canvas, and spice it up. A bundle of cinnamon sticks can contribute a touch of homespun charm, while an array of tinsel stars can add shimmer to the scene.

In fact, shiny ornaments will help draw attention to a wreath hanging in a shaded entryway. Acting as reflectors, these decorations gather what light there is and toss it about. On a balsam wreath, a fistful of jingle bells is a cheerful salutation; a simple sprig of green paired with a bell on a gossamer ribbon makes a refined accent for a city door.

Most often, the style of the house and the color of the door will dictate the choice of ribbon. The wire-edged kind is the easiest to shape into a curvaceous bow. Yet as long as the ribbon is an outdoor variety that will withstand the elements (or as long as the wreath is protected), anything goes. Plaids, stripes, and gingham—though not as traditional as plain red—are amiable partners for wreaths. Try two or more patterns together, and for a luxuriant look, leave the ends of the ribbon long so that they can flutter in the wind.

OPPOSITE: *Dangling in the center of each window, wreaths suspended by decorative ribbon create a refined and ordered look, in keeping with the formal style of the architecture. When the blinds are open, the verdant adornments afford pleasure both inside and out.*

At Christmas play and make good cheer,
For Christmas comes but once a year.

—THOMAS TUSSER

Everything we do to decorate a wreath can also be done to dress up a swag or a garland. Both swags and garlands can be partnered with wreaths or used in their stead. A rope of white pine, for instance, will drape gracefully over a doorway, along a porch railing, or around pillars and lampposts. An artful swag, the simplest decoration of all, need be no more than a fistful of greens tied at the ends with twine and left unadorned, eighteenth-century style.

The pièce de résistance? Window boxes. In many climates, the soil will not have frozen, which means that festive evergreen boughs and holly branches can be pushed into the soil easily. How about ornamental cabbages, red apples, and pineapples (the latter being a symbol of welcome) all lined up in a row? Christmas invites excess. Fill up your window boxes like harvest baskets with a bumper crop of glorious greens and fruit.

OPPOSITE: *Enlist outdoor features to join in the celebration. This charming wagon wheel, propped up against a rustic fence, becomes part of the holiday scene with a pinecone-studded wreath and a fresh coat of glistening snow.*

LEFT: *Imaginative props can enhance any setting. Positioned beside a country gate, a weather-beaten wooden chair—minus its seat—assumes a holiday demeanor when filled with greens.*

🌿 Moonstruck Props 🌿

To transform an ordinary entry or porch into a yuletide stage, bring out some eye-catching elements. An antique sled parked by the front door or a small evergreen tree in a country crock can serve as a hint of what awaits inside. Other signs of merriment include twin topiaries tied with bows, a stone (or faux stone) urn jammed with statuesque branches, and a rickety, wooden bucket filled with a cluster of red berries.

Still, nothing denotes gaiety like a portly snowman. If the weather has favored you with an abundance of white, enlist the children to help you sculpt at least one sentry to stand guard in the front yard. As a finishing touch, crown your jolly sculpture with a top hat, a halo of evergreens, or a red stocking cap.

❧ Light Show ❧

Candles are a large part of the pageantry of Christmas. Shining from the windows, they bring the exterior of a home to life. The electric or battery-operated models are the safest variety, and many have built-in sensors that turn them on at dusk and off at dawn. Picture a single flickering light glowing from the interior sill of each window. To enhance the show, loop strings of tiny white lights through the trees and along porch railings.

At party time, post luminarias (using white bags partially filled with sand) along a snowy path. Center each votive in a glass container inside the bag to keep it erect. (Luminarias, like all candles or lanterns, should be carefully watched.) On the porch, heighten the festivity with a chorus line of white paper lanterns (battery-operated lights can be used for these, too). And don't overlook your indoor Christmas tree, which can double as an outdoor decoration. Placed by a window, the light-festooned tree will seem the perfect beacon for carolers.

SILENT NIGHT

Whether we gather around the piano to join in song or go caroling from house to house, the emotional effect that holiday tunes have upon us is powerful. Fill your home with their magic by compiling a collection of your favorite CDs to play throughout the season. Or organize a carol-singing party, and invite all the neighbors.

CHAPTER TWO

A Warm Welcome

Hospitality should begin the moment we open our doors. With that in mind, let there be seasonal aromas wafting through the air, candles flickering everywhere, and music ringing through the halls. It's a well-known paradox of nature that during the winter solstice, when darkness descends and animals hibernate, our senses are most receptive. Play to this heightened sensibility, and indulge in the festivity of the season. Whether you have visitors popping in for a few hours of celebratory activities or guests who will be settling in for a few days, you'll want to make sure that above all they feel welcome. And what better way to accomplish this goal than by enveloping your friends and loved ones in the spirit of the season?

Season's Greetings

The front hall is the perfect place for a grand beginning. But grand needn't translate to ornate. An earthenware bowl of clove-studded apples and a beeswax candle centered in a tiny circle of boxwood proclaim "Merry Christmas" to all who cross the threshold.

OPPOSITE: *Decorated with a variety of red and white candles, a hall table evokes the magic of the season. Rather than stow extra candles in a cupboard, put them to use by creating an eye-catching still life.*

Fashion the hall table to serve as a prelude to the rest of the home. If yours is a relaxed country Christmas devoid of tinsel and shiny balls, wooden boxes of heady paperwhites in full bloom and baskets of pinecones will set the right tone from the start. Should the stairs be in view, wrap the railings and banisters with fresh greens and tie them with neat red bows. A potted flower arranged on each step or a collection of flowering pots on the landing will imbue the hall and surrounding area with a fresh, outdoor feeling (just make sure that your decorations don't interfere with traffic). A traditional kissing ball of bright aromatic greens, suspended from a ribbon or chain, will rival the costliest crystal chandelier, while a simple sprig of mistletoe hanging overhead will bring a smile to all who pass beneath it.

BELOW, RIGHT: *Garlands of evergreen cascading down the banisters of a staircase are finished off at the newel posts in elegant arrangements of fresh fruit and waxy green leaves.*

OPPOSITE: *On a contemporary staircase, miniature evergreen trees paired with votive candles in red glass holders put a spring in the step of residents and guests alike. (Should you try this in your own home, make sure that there is no risk of the candles being knocked over.)*

GLOBAL WARMING

Long before the tree became the centerpiece of Christmas celebrations, small presents were often attached to the kissing ball. The traditional English version of the ball is a sphere of verdant greens, candles, apples, and mistletoe. Over the years, however, variations have included all kinds of ornaments, ribbons, and tinsel. Modern renditions range from globes of fresh and faux greens to smaller, pomander-style ornaments studded with synthetic cranberries, raspberries, and leaves. Custom dictates that the kissing ball—hung just high enough to clear the head of the tallest merrymaker—should stay in place throughout the Twelve Days of Christmas.

OPPOSITE: *Lush greenery and white pillar candles— each nestled in a bed of sea glass and smooth stones— unite to create a sense of understated elegance along a staircase. Notice how the simple yet striking holiday decorations enhance rather than compete with the view.*

If you prefer, take the plunge and step up the tempo: crowd a glass compote to overflowing with gilded fruits and nuts, and center it on that antique tavern table. Flank the compote with etched-glass hurricane lamps to increase the sparkle factor. In lieu of conventional Christmas items, rely on long-legged white amaryllis—five or six pots, with or without lavish satin bows—to bedazzle visitors.

You can really greet your guests with a warm welcome by literally warming them up. After all, it's cold out there in the dark. A punch bowl or a crock of hot mulled cider stationed on the hall table makes it a snap to offer guests a cup as soon as they remove their coats and mittens. The spicy

RIGHT: *Celebrate the bounty of nature with an easy-to-put-together tableau of color and texture.*

OPPOSITE: *A bouquet of flowers set atop a glass cake stand filled with holiday treats makes for a dramatic—and mouthwatering—presentation. Make sure the plate stays full so that guests can help themselves as they come and go.*

grog will taste every bit as good as it smells. Load a decorative tray with an array of cellophane-wrapped cookies or jars of your special spicy jam. Homemade delicacies or small wrapped gifts heaped in a basket can act as decorations as well as favors to hand out to friends when they depart. It's a well-known Christmas canon: visitors must never leave empty-handed.

COMMON SCENTS

Fill your home with the scents of the season. In addition to bringing in armloads of aromatic greens (laurel is particularly fragrant), simmer citrus peel, nutmeg, cloves, cinnamon sticks, ginger, and water in a small saucepan on the stove. Subtly scented candles—whether peppermint, pine, or vanilla—can also help to infuse the air with the fragrances of the holiday.

✺ Corner Warmers ✺

Provide visitors with a delightful surprise by giving the powder room a holiday flair. Even a small gesture, such as a stack of holiday-themed hand towels, will go a long way. For something a bit more pervasive—yet still relatively easy to accomplish—transform your powder room into an enchanting winter wonderland by employing an all-white color scheme. Hang up your grandmother's lace-edged white hand towels, and float white candles in clear glass cylinders. A dish of white soaps embossed with snowflakes and a pristine jug of white roses will also provide visually arresting touches.

Should a cozy motif be the order of the day, turn up the heat. Nestle a colorful soap redolent of the season by the sink. Bright embroidered hand towels piled in a basket and a vase of vibrant flowers—red tulips, begonias, a branch of azalea—will lift the spirits, while a Christmas-themed rug will complete the scene.

✺ Comfort and Joy ✺

Overnight guests and Christmas are synonymous. Your visitors will appreciate your efforts to make them feel at home, but why not go one better? 'Tis the season, after all, for giving, and what better gift than to make your guests' holiday stay as enjoyable as possible?

To enhance the guest room, begin with the bed. It should be as inviting to look at as it is conducive to visions of sugarplums. A cozy, holiday-patterned bedspread and mounds of accent pillows—the quickest means for changing the look of any bedroom—will be a welcome sight for a

OPPOSITE: *In a guest bedroom, a cozy quilt, a canopy of heady greens, and a small aromatic tree issue a heart-warming welcome.*

weary traveler. Lay a favorite needlepoint pillow—one with a Christmas design—at the head of the bed. Or pile on decorative throw pillows covered in rich tartan plaid. Reiterate by employing a similar plaid for the duvet cover. And layer, layer, layer! An antique quilt, an extra lamb's-wool blanket (make it red), and a soft throw can unite to envelop your visitors in the sense of luxury that comes from an abundance of comfort.

SWEET DREAMS

Since it is the season to pamper the people we love, why not treat them to some cozy flannel sheets? Turn down the covers, tuck a sweet sachet of subtle spices and lavender under a pillow, and leave a gift of comfy linen slippers beside the bed.

Once the bed has been suitably decked out, turn your attention to the nightstand. A silver water pitcher and a pair of drinking glasses are thoughtful additions, regardless of the time of year. But for Christmas, why not also include a bowl of red and green apples, which will not only bring holiday color to the mix, but also provide something for nocturnal nibbling. Add a leather-bound volume of Christmas poems for bedtime reading and a vase of fresh flowers to complete the scene.

There are numerous other ways to infuse a bedroom with the revelry of the season. Hang a fresh garland or a stately wreath above the bed. Or stand a fanciful Victorian-style feather tree on the chest by the door.

OPPOSITE: *Simple touches speak volumes—like this jolly stocking tied to a bedpost. Stir up the Christmas hospitality even further by stationing a dish of traditional shortbread cookies on the nightstand for a bedtime snack.*

LEFT: *Anything goes: roses, citrus slices, cinnamon sticks, ivy. This sweet-scented still life evokes a holiday feel without using the more traditional recipe of evergreens and holly berries. In lieu of a candle, a kerosene lamp sheds a warm glow.*

Share surplus ornaments with your guests as well. Tie a gleaming Christmas ball to a bedpost with an antique ribbon, or lay several ornaments out for view on a silver tray atop the dresser. One red bow on a perfume bottle holding a sprig of ivy will imbue the entire dressing table with holiday cheer. And a music box that plays a well-known Christmas tune will be an entertaining and heartwarming surprise.

The joy that you give to others
Is the joy that comes back to you.

—JOHN GREENLEAF WHITTIER

CHAPTER THREE

The Heart of the Home

We all have a particular space in which we like to gather. For some it may be the relaxed, perfect-for-entertaining great room; for others it may be the living room with its breathtaking view of the lake; still others might gravitate toward the laid-back family room where the kids stretch out on the rug to do their reading. Almost always, this cherished gathering place is the site for the main tree—the tree that's adorned with our most treasured ornaments. We unpack our rainbow collection of trimmings, and with each unveiling of tissue, another memory is awakened. A tree decked with homemade trinkets, gifts from friends, and eclectic travel souvenirs is the epitome of Christmas. On every bough hangs a reminder of something or somebody we love.

Yet there are many other ways to dress up a tree. Depending upon our style preferences, a Christmas tree can be as plain as a brown egg or as fancy and frilly as a wedding cake. We can do as we please with as many trees—one by the hearth, perhaps a table-size version in the kitchen—as we please. And Oh Tannenbaum!, what possibilities.

OPPOSITE: *Vintage-style Father Christmas figures and a sprinkling of plaid bows lend a tree an old-fashioned flavor. Since an empty, nonworking fireplace would have made a rather cold backdrop, the owners have filled the hearth with holly.*

❦ The Family Tree ❦

Henry David Thoreau cut down a spruce and decorated it with white candles for his home at Walden Pond. Lovely in itself, a tree doesn't require much to earn our admiration. Imagine a stately, au naturel tree today. Banishing all notions of electric lights or anything artificial, the owners have threaded the branches with garlands of cranberries and popcorn strung on the spot. In lieu of glass ornaments, there are autumn leaves pressed as flat as paper, woven willow orbs, and such edible decorations as gingerbread men and sugar-dusted hearts. From bits of ribbon or colored string hang dried flowers such as yarrow, hydrangeas, pearly everlastings, and roses. Cinnamon sticks and miniature baskets brimming with cloves delight the nose as well as the eye. Casually attired as it is, this anything-but-plain-Jane conifer would be as handsome in a penthouse as in a farmhouse.

BELOW, RIGHT: *Fashioned from seedpods, twigs, dried flowers, and tiny gilded pinecones and acorns, an all-natural ornament is dazzling in its own right. Carefully stored, the artful decoration will endure for years.*

OPPOSITE: *Forget the lights and tinsel. Handsomely decorated cookies, tied on with unassuming ribbon, possess their own homespun appeal. In assorted colors and patterns, the sweets are a testament to the baker's talent.*

Still, holiday enthusiasm promotes flamboyance. A vast, ceiling-grazing tree might very well warrant a flood of silver icicles and legions of brilliant gold ornaments. A two-tone color theme delivers a bigger punch than a swirl of color—especially when both the evergreen and the room are large; the eye has less reason to flit tiresomely from object to object. And any combination of two colors will have a powerful effect, from silver and blue to red and green to purple and gold.

Paring down the palette further, you could fashion a flight of fancy that calls upon only one color. A twelve-foot (3.5m) tree adorned with oversize ornaments—from balls to snowflakes—in an iridescent palette of white evokes thoughts of a snow-covered forest. In such a situation, tiny white lights—reminiscent of stars—make for the perfect finishing touch.

Often overlooked in the planning, tree toppers and tree stands are part of the final picture. Angels and cherubs rate high for the former, but there's leeway for ingenuity here as well. A giant bow placed at a tree's pinnacle lets fall glorious streamers, on all sides, to the floor. A luminous gold star is reminiscent of the star that shone above the

OPPOSITE: *A gold color scheme is an elegant choice for a Christmas tree. Here, ornaments in varying shapes and sizes create visual interest, making the monochromatic display anything but dull. A large, golden star shines from the top of the tall tree, contributing to the overall luminescence.*

EVERGREEN

Think ahead to next year's gift list, and recycle some of the needles from this year's tree to fashion perfumed pillows and sachets. According to folklore, we should also pack one small piece of the tree away with our decorations for good luck.

stable on that holy night. Nonetheless, for high drama, nothing comes close to a prism-laden chandelier. Should you be fortunate to have one, designers often recommend placing the tree in the center of the room and letting the chandelier serve as a celestial topper.

On the other end, the ubiquitous metal tree stand is less than interesting. Search for an old or reproduction cast-iron model. As an alternative, plunk the tree in a metal washtub, a clay pot, or a copper bucket. Or use an ordinary plastic bucket to hold water and hide the bucket inside a wicker basket. If you plan to use a tree skirt (a strategically stacked pile of small white birch logs will work, too), don't settle for a hokey cloth. Insist on something of note—a vintage tablecloth, a plaid blanket, a silk sari throw. Creatively wrapped presents are also part of the under-the-tree decoration. They can tie in with the theme of the tree, or they can make a visual statement of their very own.

THEME TRIMMINGS

In recent years, theme trees—like theme parties—have grown more popular. A child's tree might be decked out with candy canes and cookies, farm animals fashioned from felt, dollhouse furniture, and paper cutouts. A mitten tree would be just that: a little tree covered in whimsical, child-size felt and knit mittens held on with ribbon or wooden clothespins. And at the very top? A superlative mitten pointing straight up to the sky.

RIGHT: *A palette of purple and gold can imbue a Christmas tree with a regal air.*

OPPOSITE: *Favorite storybook characters have their place at Christmas. What little girl wouldn't love a child-size tree championed by Madeline? Notice the Eiffel Tower on top.*

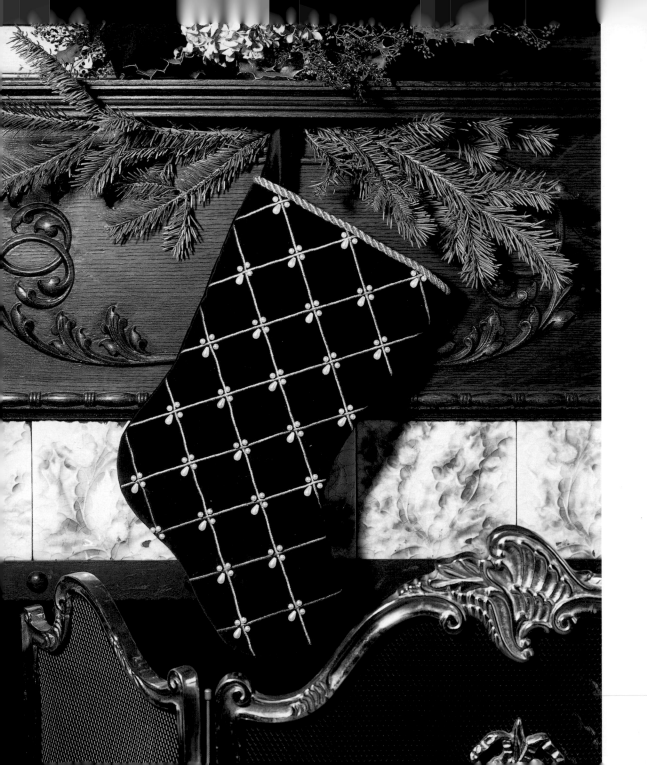

❧ Hearthside Pleasures ❧

Mantelpieces are as versatile as wreaths and trees. Traditional or contemporary, done up to the nines or homespun, each should be a part of the festivities. Pull out the stops and fabricate an opulent assemblage of greens and ribbons. Or set a holiday tone with just a few well-placed accents. Stockings, filled with anticipation and hung in a row, are the customary decoration. A clothesline (complete with wooden pins) on which Christmas cards are displayed is another old-time favorite. Study the scene for inspiration.

OPPOSITE: *A red velvet stocking makes a classic statement on a dignified mantel.*

BELOW, LEFT: *Stockings are the time-honored form of mantel decoration, but why stop there? Greens interspersed with nutcracker figures and candy canes not only enhance the display, but also bring out the child in each of us.*

You may want to design your mantelscape to fit in with the overall style of your home. Evergreen branches—accented with colorful nutcracker figures, fragrant fruit, and pinecones—are compatible with a traditional setting. And some of the best-dressed Colonial-style houses wear lemons, pineapples, and lady apples along their mantels. But any sort of vegetable, fruit, or other humble natural treasure—such as moss, stones, or leaves—can step up to claim a place on the mantel. Topiaries—lanky myrtles potted ankle-deep in reindeer moss or a stout pair of boxwoods in hand-painted cachepots—make stunning graphic touches.

If yours is a modern mantel where art is displayed, combine your treasures with seasonal trappings. A collection of framed black-and-white photographs, for instance, requires minimal adjustment. A smattering of white candles set on silver dishes—perhaps paired with a glass bauble or two—is all that's necessary to create a low-key holiday ambience (just make sure that the flames don't threaten to damage the art). To double the viewer's delight, balance a gold-framed mirror or two behind the glittery display.

> *Heap on more wood!—the wind is chill;*
> *But let it whistle as it will,*
> *We'll keep our Christmas merry still.*
>
> —SIR WALTER SCOTT

The same sort of understated elegance is easy to achieve with white plants and flowers. Pots of paperwhites, amaryllis, calla lilies, roses, and sweet-scented freesia are perfect for conjuring up a sophisticated, wintry tone—especially when used with glass or silver. Line them up on the mantel and they'll steal the show. With this scenario, the row of stockings should be white—each with a different lace trim. If an all-white display seems too stark for your liking, combine the white flowers with branches of greens, pussy willows, and berries. Realistic faux berries will withstand the heat and maintain their color best.

Candles, which come in a wide variety of styles and hues, not only make eye-catching decorative accents, but can create a riveting display all on their own. Candles in such holiday shapes as pinecones, snowmen, and Christmas trees are a cheerful windfall, capable of bringing a touch of whimsy to the setting. For a bit more show and glitter, try candles with a pearlized or metallic finish. Handmade botanical candles that include rose petals, herbs, or twigs within their translucent walls fare especially well when the emphasis is on natural decorations. As the center burns down, the petals and plants become more apparent.

A forest of white or cream-colored candles forms a breathtaking focal point. To heighten the visual interest of such a display, select an assortment of shapes and heights—including pillars, votives, cubes, and balls—and group them together.

If you prefer a more colorful declaration that Christmas is here, create an arrangement of cranberry-colored candles. For a stately effect,

OPPOSITE: *A straightforward presentation of natural ingredients evocative of the season—no extra frills, bows, or baubles—is always memorable. Twin urns help to unify the display without seeming too fancy.*

ONCE UPON A TIME

Christmas stories—especially when read by the light of the tree or beside a roaring fire—are a source of delight for all. Placing a stack of your favorite tomes on display encourages the revisiting of well-loved holiday tales that are neglected during the rest of the year. Some traditional favorites include Truman Capote's A Christmas Memory, *O. Henry's* The Gift of the Magi, *and* Christmas in Maine *by Robert P. Tristam Coffin. Little children will also appreciate suggestions. Beside a child-size rocker, plant a basket of classics including* The Fir Tree *by Hans Christian Andersen and* Once on Christmas *by Dorothy Thompson.*

fit spiraled red tapers into candelabras stationed at either end of the mantel. Or place the tapers in individual brass candlesticks. Gathered en masse, the candlesticks will be twice as effective as they would be if scattered about the living room. Add a couple of lemons at their bases or a simple string of cranberry glass beads, and the mood is set. Alternating translucent red and green glass votive holders forms a Christmas-like caravan that can carry a room.

Roasting chestnuts or not, guests will notice details, so give the hearth a face-lift. Polish the andirons and the fireplace tools. Pinecones in a wire basket, a copper tub, or a leather bucket make an attractive accent and come in handy (as do candle stubs) when starting a fire. An

iron pillar holder that will accommodate six to eight pillar candles suggests the blaze of a Yule log in a nonworking fireplace. The glow of the candles mimics firelight minus the worry of lugging logs and sweeping up ashes. In a sumptuous setting, a filigreed brass fire screen will veil the burning logs without obliterating the dancing light.

🌿 Table Talk 🌿

From coffee tables to end tables and side tables, all sorts of surfaces in our gathering areas provide opportunities for Christmas still lifes. Rather than leave that pine stand by the sofa bare and sulky, we can designate it as the perfect spot for an enormous glass canister filled with reflective tear-shaped ornaments or a wooden birdhouse with a teeny wreath at its door.

GREENERY

Savvy gardeners often visit garden centers and nurseries in search of small landscape plants that can be used indoors as refreshing decorations. Later, the baby boxwoods and evergreens can be moved to the yard and planted. Rather than tossing out our cut Christmas trees with the trash, we can recycle them for the garden as well. Tree branches can be used as a protective winter blanket on beds and borders, or the entire tree can be put through a tree shredder to form mulch.

OPPOSITE:

Windowsills are lovely roosting places for votives. Here, the candles are joined by greens, berries, and pinecones, which bring a touch of the country to the city view.

Flowers are jolts of color for us to scatter about. Tulips and ranunculuses are two favorites, but even carnations gain appeal when short-stemmed and bunched. Certain potted plants, if treated like cut flowers, also yield pleasing results. Experiment with a lone poinsettia in a vase or a single red amaryllis and three red roses. Miniature trees in decorative pots lend themselves well to groupings on larger tables. In a room without a tree, try fitting wee evergreens with miniature lights.

Family photographs of Christmases past are fuel for many hours of conversation. Arrange framed pictures on tables where they can easily be viewed. Stack photograph albums—all about Christmas—on the coffee table. Put out dozens of holiday snapshots (the ones you always meant to frame) in a silver bowl for the family to rifle through by the fire.

Window Dressing

Windows are ideal spots for showcasing all sorts of riches. Even a diminutive window in a seaside cottage features a sliver of shelf for resting an offbeat ornament or a demitasse saucer of holiday potpourri. If the sill allows, a beribboned pot of trailing ivy or pots of paperwhites will thrive at the window.

In lieu of a candle, dangle a white origami snowflake or dove in front of the glass. Or replace the pull on the shade—just for the holiday season—with a light-catching, handblown Christmas ornament. A small wreath suspended on the inside of the window will be enjoyed by passersby as well as by company.

Curtain tiebacks can also be festive. Dig into your bag of gift-wrapping trim and see what inspires you. Gold twine, ribbon, and glass beads all have decorative potential. If you prefer, go the natural route. Twist a garland of ivy around the curtain, or fashion a circlet of green and attach pinecone rosettes. Bare windows take on a whole new persona when draped with evergreen garlands.

OPPOSITE: *A wire plant stand filled with a trio of small evergreens—each with a star at its top—becomes a glorious enhancement for an undressed window.*

EAT, DRINK, AND BE MERRY

As you gather around with company, you're bound to want to share some savory treats. A tray outfitted with a silver or china tea set is a pleasing tabletop reminder that we owe ourselves and our guests a respite. When cups and saucers are at the ready, it's no chore to put on the kettle. Anticipating visitors, we can add a glass jar of cookies or a tin of buttery shortbread to the vignette. A portable bar set in a sea grass basket or atop a lacquered tray is another plus. Include holiday coasters or cocktail napkins and a glass cylinder of lemons and limes for color.

CHAPTER FOUR

A Feast for the Eye

Once the presents have been opened and the flurry of wrapping paper has settled, it's time for the feast. Many of our happiest holiday memories revolve around Christmas dinner—the lively conversations we've shared and the savory food in which we've indulged. This annual event can be made all the more memorable by jazzing up the setting. From the table to the sideboard to the chandelier, there are numerous opportunities for injecting holiday spirit.

Setting the Stage

Whether you're planning a boisterous buffet lunch or an intimate midnight supper, it helps to set the table long before family members and guests assemble. The most successful settings are ones where the linens, dishes, glassware, and centerpieces all complement one another. When it comes to linens, remember to think about not only the tablecloth, but the napkins as well. If you have a beautiful table that you want to show off, opt for a runner instead of a cloth. Place mats—

OPPOSITE: *From the tartan plaid tablecloth to the Christmas china, this festive table exclaims "Happy Holidays." Simple flourishes—such as the cranberries in the vase and the red bow and jingle bells tied around each napkin—are bound to form a lasting impression.*

OPPOSITE: *Red and white flowers beckon guests to a relaxed holiday buffet. Boughs of holly scattered about the table enhance the scene, as do votives tucked inside translucent red holders.*

which provide a great opportunity for bringing colorful accents to the table—can perform their humble service in conjunction with or in the absence of a full-length table covering. They are also a fine means for safeguarding an antique tablecloth.

When deciding upon the look of your table, start by picking a color scheme. If you have special holiday china that you bring out every year or heirloom accessories—perhaps Grandmother's damask table-cloth—that are a traditional part of the celebration, then build your palette around these beloved pieces. After all, sharing the treasures that have been in the family for generations is just another gift we extend to our guests.

DINNER IS SERVED

Feeding the people we love is a ceremony in itself. To ease the pressure of getting everything on the table at the same time, call upon an age-old strategy: divide and conquer. For starters, pass trays of soup—with pastry lids—to be eaten by the fire. Dinner and dessert can then be staged buffet-style in the dining room. Plan dishes that can be made ahead of time. Or choose forgiving recipes, such as succulent roast pork with herbs, that won't fall apart should you run late. An assortment of finger foods and a glazed ham are easy on the cook. And always accept a friend's offer to help or bring something.

An all-white theme, accented by some greenery or touches of gold, will create a white Christmas—regardless of the weather outside. For an elegant look, try a crisp white tablecloth joined by gold-rimmed white china, gold-rimmed glasses, and golden linen napkins. Patterns— whether on napkins, hand-painted china, or crystal flutes—play especially well on a sea of white.

The time-honored Christmas colors—green and red—are also versatile in that they can be called upon to create a stately tone or a less formal mood. A forest green tablecloth, cream-colored china, tartan plaid napkins, and cranberry-colored goblets can all unite to form a traditional-looking spread. For something a little more footloose and fancy-free, lay down a white cloth and alternate plates of red and green. Top every red plate with a green napkin and every green plate with a red napkin.

OPPOSITE: *From the dishes to the linens, there are all sorts of opportunities for bringing holiday color to the table. Christmas miniatures, such as this painted rocking horse, provide delightful accents.*

CHRISTMASES PAST

Search tag sales, antiques stores, and consignment shops for vintage glassware that lends itself to a holiday table. Translucent green Depression glass (manufactured from about 1920 to 1940) is one Noel-appropriate variety. Picture a leaf-colored glass plate under a small white saucer of Christmas plum pudding. Ubiquitous milk glass, which is still being manufactured in dozens of configurations, marries blissfully with the green leaves and red berries of holly.

Keep in mind that everything does not need to match. While a beautifully set formal table with the correct accoutrements is an impressive and wondrous sight, so too is a less rigid design where some of the dishes may be of one pattern and some of another. The latter situation works best, though, if there is some unifying element, such as a shared color.

❧ The Center of Attention ❧

The centerpiece will be the real attention-grabber at the table. Whether your display is an elegant tiered stand filled with glistening sugared grapes or a crystal bowl packed with a compact, domed arrangement of lush red roses, be sure to use only the freshest ingredients. But don't feel restricted to natural components. A clear, shallow bowl filled with shiny glass ornaments is sure to create a dazzling display. Just keep in mind that you don't want your centerpiece to be so tall or large that it hinders conversation. If you're looking for height, include something unobtrusive like a thin, curly willow tip. For a gala evening dinner, use a slender, pedestal-shaped vase that will hold blooms aloft and out of the way.

Old wisdom cautions that a long, rectangular arrangement works better on a long table and that a round piece fares best on a round table. But again, there are no hard-and-fast rules, so follow your intuition. A low, artful display that winds its way down the length of a rectangular table or an arrangement that entails the placement of individual bud

OPPOSITE: *Sometimes less is best. Eschewing a garish centerpiece, this table finds an amiable companion in an uncomplicated basket of fresh greens. A tiny glass ornament and a sprig of greenery atop each plate are enough to say Christmas.*

vases at each setting can create a scene that is much more pleasing to the eye than a single bouquet. For a quick fix, lay green branches or boughs of crab apple down the middle of the table. At intervals alongside the fruit or intermingled with the greens, place thick candles (just make sure that there's no chance of a stray leaf coming into contact with a flame). If a streamlined design is more to your liking, employ a row of miniature poinsettias, each set in a gleaming silver julep cup. For a rustic look, a miniature terra-cotta pot—painted with a cheerful holiday emblem and filled with a votive—positioned just beyond each place setting will bring a warm glow to each of your guests.

In fact, with its celebratory air and understated elegance, candlelight is a holiday requisite. (No matter that a candle flame is also said to sharpen the wit and ignite conversation.) Depending on what works best with your tablescape, assemble clusters of votives in holders embellished with beads, or group candlesticks of brass or crystal together. Candlesticks encircled with tendrils of ivy and bright berries seem even more festive. And beds of dried flowers and fruit elevate plain white candles to glorious heights. On more modern tables, water

OPPOSITE: *A theme of winter white can bring glamour to a holiday table. White roses surrounded by greens unite with tall, fluted votive holders for a stylish look. In candlelight, a table such as this will seem as effervescent as champagne.*

I will honor Christmas in my heart, and try to keep it all the year.

—CHARLES DICKENS

OPPOSITE:

*Stationing a minia-
ture house at each
place setting pro-
vides friends and
family with an
unexpected treat.
But such uplifting
decorations need
not stand alone.
Complemented by
tea lights and nap-
kin rings, they
become even more
appealing.*

enhances the glow. Launch whole flotillas of candles in shallow bowls for a warm but contemporary look. These days, floating candles come in a variety of shapes, from snowflakes to peppermint candies.

Keep in mind that color has the power to dramatize light—just think of the effect that stained glass has. For more vibrant illumination, post small tea-light lamps with jewel-tone beaded shades around the centerpiece or at either end of the table. Or drop tea lights, ball candles, or votives inside colorful glass holders. In soft candlelight, clear glass vases filled with cranberries seem to glow (the cranberries also help to anchor unruly flower stems in water). True, hollowed-out apples—each fitted with a burning votive—don't seem to blaze from within like glass, but the glowing red of the fruit in candlelight exudes natural splendor.

COLLECTIBLES À LA CARTE

With a captive audience on hand, collectors are advised to show off their treasures, such as wooden crèche figures, miniature houses, old-fashioned tin toys, and cherubs. Overlook the peeling paint and the bits of rust—they're part of the appeal of these prized possessions. Accented with greens and votives, an antique flock of tiny carved sheep is folksy and charming. Put well-loved trinkets to work, too. An antique toy sleigh can be piled with mints or nuts.

🌾 Delightful Details 🌾

Napkin rings always bring something extra to the table. Candidates range from ribbon or raffia to a stretchy string of little bells. In fact, any material that twists easily or any object that has an opening through which a napkin could slide, such as a cookie cutter, will do. Tuck a small flower or a holly sprig under the tie, or attach some other sort of treat— perhaps an antique button, a charm, or a piece of Christmas candy. Browse through catalogs for napkin rings with a holiday or winter theme, such as an angel, a snowflake, or a wreath.

For a personal touch, award each guest a tiny place card. A smooth stone, a green leaf, and a wedge of cedar shingle are just a few

OPPOSITE: *Just a few thoughtful gestures can go a long way to making guests feel special. Here, such hospitable details include a charming place card, a net-encased favor, and a golden cord looped loosely around the flatware and linen napkin.*

LEFT: *A simple decorative statement can have a powerful impact. Here, a fanned napkin—held in place by a single golden cord with a red tassel—creates an elegant invitation to dine.*

Everyone ends up chatting in the kitchen. Render yours merrier with a few well-placed touches. Here, meandering ivy, a simple white pitcher filled with greens and berries, and a trio of red and white pot holders interject a jubilant note.

of the possibilities for designating a seat. All it takes is a gold paint-pen to inscribe a name across the surface. But whether we go for glitzy, quaint, or funny, our place card holders should coordinate with the rest of the elements. Imagination is key: balance a place card in the leaves of an artichoke, tie one to a bunch of bright red cherries, or glue one to a blossoming twig. Tree ornaments also make great place designators. Simply tie a thick ribbon in the ornament's loop, and use that gold pen to write the name on the trailing fabric.

To make your diners feel special, drop an unexpected favor atop each plate or beside each place setting. How about stationing a kitschy snow globe or a Christmas cracker next to each wineglass? Nutcracker figures can make amusing treats for young children, and tree ornaments used as place cards can double as gifts for guests to take home.

FOOD FOR THOUGHT

Since you'll probably be spending a good amount of time in the kitchen over the holidays—and since this is the area to which everyone gravitates anyway—go ahead and give this room a dose of holiday cheer. Bring in a pitcher of red and white flowers, or if space is at a premium, hang a swag of greenery at the kitchen window. Another space-efficient trick is to replace everyday canisters—whether they hold cookies or utensils— with holiday-themed containers.

RIGHT: *A playful stocking decorated with gingerbread men and candy canes looks at home in a kitchen window. To further the theme, a troop of bite-size gingerbread people lines up along the mullions.*

OPPOSITE: *Decorated with snowy white icing, star- and bell-shaped cookies make fine ornaments. Poke a hole in each before baking to make stringing easier.*